50 Weekend Wins Recipes

By: Kelly Johnson

Table of Contents

- Pulled Pork Sliders
- BBQ Chicken Pizza
- Beef Tacos with Lime Crema
- Chicken Alfredo Pasta Bake
- Loaded Nachos
- Grilled Steak Frites
- Buffalo Cauliflower Bites
- Shakshuka
- Shrimp and Grits
- Veggie Stir-Fry with Tofu
- Mac and Cheese with Bacon
- Grilled Veggie Platter with Hummus
- Carne Asada Burritos
- Meatball Sub Sandwiches
- Spaghetti Carbonara
- BBQ Ribs with Coleslaw
- Paella

- Sweet and Sour Chicken
- Crispy Fish Tacos
- Lobster Rolls
- Baked Ziti with Sausage
- Salmon with Avocado Salsa
- Chicken Parmesan
- Mediterranean Lamb Kebabs
- Goulash
- Beef Wellington
- Cajun Jambalaya
- Spicy BBQ Pulled Chicken Nachos
- Mushroom Risotto
- Grilled Shrimp Skewers
- Spicy Chicken Wings
- Baked Sweet Potatoes with Sour Cream
- Grilled Flatbreads with Pesto
- Philly Cheesesteak Sandwiches
- Steak and Potato Salad
- Classic Beef Burgers

- Shrimp Scampi
- Veggie Pizza
- Steak Tacos with Guacamole
- Tomato Basil Soup with Grilled Cheese
- Chicken and Dumplings
- Slow-Cooker Chili
- Beef Tostadas
- Ramen with Soft Boiled Eggs
- Loaded Baked Potatoes
- Banh Mi Sandwiches
- Carne Asada Fries
- Stuffed Bell Peppers
- Grilled Cheese with Tomato Jam
- Chicken Shawarma Wraps

Pulled Pork Sliders

Tender pulled pork on soft slider buns, topped with tangy slaw.
Ingredients:

- 2 lbs pork shoulder
- 1 cup BBQ sauce
- 1/2 cup apple cider vinegar
- 1 tbsp brown sugar
- 1 onion, chopped
- 2 cloves garlic, minced
- 1 tbsp paprika
- 1 tbsp cumin
- Salt and pepper to taste
- Slider buns
- Coleslaw (optional topping)

Instructions:

1. Season the pork shoulder with paprika, cumin, salt, and pepper.
2. Place pork in a slow cooker with onion, garlic, apple cider vinegar, brown sugar, and BBQ sauce.
3. Cook on low for 8 hours, or until the pork is tender and easily shreds.
4. Shred the pork using two forks and toss in the remaining sauce.

5. Serve the pulled pork on slider buns with optional coleslaw.

BBQ Chicken Pizza

Grilled BBQ chicken with a smoky, sweet sauce on a crispy pizza crust.

Ingredients:

- 1 lb chicken breast, cooked and shredded
- 1/2 cup BBQ sauce
- 1 pizza dough (store-bought or homemade)
- 1/2 cup red onion, thinly sliced
- 1/2 cup cilantro, chopped
- 1 1/2 cups shredded mozzarella cheese
- 1/2 cup gouda cheese, shredded

Instructions:

1. Preheat oven to 475°F. Roll out the pizza dough on a floured surface.
2. Mix the shredded chicken with BBQ sauce.
3. Spread a thin layer of BBQ sauce on the pizza dough.
4. Top with BBQ chicken, red onion, mozzarella, and gouda.
5. Bake for 12-15 minutes until the crust is golden and cheese is bubbly.
6. Garnish with chopped cilantro and serve.

Beef Tacos with Lime Crema

Ground beef seasoned with spices, topped with a creamy lime sauce.

Ingredients for Beef:

- 1 lb ground beef
- 1 tsp cumin
- 1 tsp chili powder
- 1 tsp garlic powder
- Salt and pepper to taste
- 1 tbsp olive oil
- 8 small taco shells

Ingredients for Lime Crema:

- 1/2 cup sour cream
- 2 tbsp lime juice
- 1 tbsp cilantro, chopped
- Salt to taste

Instructions:

1. Heat olive oil in a skillet over medium heat. Add ground beef and cook until browned.
2. Stir in cumin, chili powder, garlic powder, salt, and pepper. Cook for another 2-3 minutes.

3. In a small bowl, mix sour cream, lime juice, cilantro, and salt to make the lime crema.

4. Warm the taco shells and fill with the seasoned beef.

5. Drizzle lime crema over the tacos and serve with additional toppings if desired.

Chicken Alfredo Pasta Bake

A creamy, cheesy chicken Alfredo pasta bake with a golden, bubbly topping.

Ingredients:

- 2 cups cooked chicken breast, cubed
- 12 oz penne pasta, cooked
- 2 cups heavy cream
- 1 cup shredded parmesan cheese
- 1 cup shredded mozzarella cheese
- 1/2 cup breadcrumbs
- 1 tbsp olive oil
- 1 garlic clove, minced
- Salt and pepper to taste

Instructions:

1. Preheat oven to 375°F.
2. In a large skillet, heat olive oil and sauté garlic until fragrant. Add heavy cream and bring to a simmer.
3. Stir in the parmesan cheese and season with salt and pepper.
4. In a baking dish, combine the cooked pasta, cubed chicken, and Alfredo sauce.
5. Top with mozzarella cheese and breadcrumbs.
6. Bake for 20-25 minutes until the top is golden and bubbly.

Loaded Nachos

Crispy tortilla chips topped with cheese, sour cream, jalapeños, and other tasty toppings.

Ingredients:

- 1 bag tortilla chips
- 2 cups shredded cheddar cheese
- 1 cup shredded mozzarella cheese
- 1/2 cup sour cream
- 1/4 cup jalapeños, sliced
- 1/2 cup diced tomatoes
- 1/4 cup green onions, chopped
- 1/2 cup guacamole (optional)
- 1/2 cup cooked ground beef or chicken (optional)

Instructions:

1. Preheat oven to 375°F.
2. Spread the tortilla chips on a baking sheet.
3. Top with shredded cheddar and mozzarella cheese.
4. Bake for 10-12 minutes, until the cheese is melted and bubbly.
5. Top with sour cream, jalapeños, tomatoes, green onions, and guacamole.
6. Serve warm.

Grilled Steak Frites

Juicy grilled steak served with crispy, golden fries.

Ingredients for Steak:

- 2 ribeye steaks (or your preferred cut)
- 2 tbsp olive oil
- Salt and pepper to taste
- 1 tbsp fresh rosemary (optional)

Ingredients for Frites:

- 4 large potatoes, peeled and cut into thin fries
- 1 tbsp olive oil
- Salt and pepper to taste

Instructions:

1. Preheat grill to medium-high heat. Rub the steaks with olive oil, salt, pepper, and rosemary.
2. Grill steaks for about 4-5 minutes on each side for medium-rare, or longer to your desired doneness.
3. For the frites, preheat oven to 425°F. Toss potato fries in olive oil, salt, and pepper.
4. Spread fries on a baking sheet and bake for 25-30 minutes, flipping halfway through.
5. Serve the grilled steak with frites on the side.

Buffalo Cauliflower Bites

Crispy, spicy cauliflower bites served with creamy blue cheese dressing.

Ingredients:

- 1 head of cauliflower, cut into florets
- 1 cup flour
- 1 tsp paprika
- 1/2 tsp garlic powder
- 1/2 tsp cayenne pepper
- 1 cup buffalo sauce
- 1/2 cup blue cheese dressing

Instructions:

1. Preheat oven to 400°F.
2. In a bowl, mix flour, paprika, garlic powder, and cayenne pepper. Toss cauliflower florets in the mixture.
3. Arrange the cauliflower on a baking sheet and bake for 25-30 minutes until crispy.
4. Toss the cauliflower in buffalo sauce and bake for an additional 5-7 minutes.
5. Serve with blue cheese dressing on the side.

Shakshuka

A hearty Middle Eastern dish with poached eggs in a spicy tomato sauce.

Ingredients:

- 2 tbsp olive oil
- 1 onion, chopped
- 2 cloves garlic, minced
- 1 bell pepper, chopped
- 1 can (14 oz) diced tomatoes
- 1 tsp cumin
- 1 tsp paprika
- Salt and pepper to taste
- 4-6 eggs
- Fresh parsley for garnish

Instructions:

1. Heat olive oil in a skillet and sauté onions, garlic, and bell pepper until soft.
2. Add the tomatoes, cumin, paprika, salt, and pepper. Simmer for 10-15 minutes.
3. Create small wells in the sauce and crack the eggs into them.
4. Cover the skillet and cook for 5-8 minutes until the eggs are poached.
5. Garnish with parsley and serve with pita or crusty bread.

Shrimp and Grits

Creamy grits topped with succulent shrimp in a savory sauce.

Ingredients for Shrimp:

- 1 lb shrimp, peeled and deveined
- 2 tbsp butter
- 2 cloves garlic, minced
- 1 tsp smoked paprika
- Salt and pepper to taste

Ingredients for Grits:

- 1 cup grits
- 4 cups water
- 2 tbsp butter
- 1 cup cheddar cheese (optional)

Instructions:

1. For the grits: Bring water to a boil and stir in grits. Reduce heat to low and cook for 20 minutes, stirring occasionally.
2. Stir in butter and cheese (if using), then season with salt and pepper.
3. For the shrimp: Heat butter in a pan and sauté garlic until fragrant. Add shrimp, paprika, salt, and pepper.
4. Cook shrimp for 2-3 minutes on each side until pink.

5. Serve shrimp on top of grits.

Veggie Stir-Fry with Tofu

Colorful vegetables and tofu stir-fried in a savory sauce.

Ingredients:

- 1 block firm tofu, cubed
- 1 cup broccoli florets
- 1 bell pepper, sliced
- 1 carrot, julienned
- 2 tbsp soy sauce
- 1 tbsp sesame oil
- 1 tsp ginger, grated
- 2 tbsp hoisin sauce

Instructions:

1. Press tofu to remove excess water, then cube it.
2. Heat sesame oil in a wok or large pan. Stir-fry tofu until golden and crispy, then set aside.
3. In the same pan, stir-fry broccoli, bell pepper, and carrot until tender.
4. Add tofu back into the pan with soy sauce, ginger, and hoisin sauce. Stir well to coat.
5. Serve hot, garnished with sesame seeds or green onions if desired.

Mac and Cheese with Bacon

A creamy, cheesy mac and cheese topped with crispy bacon bits.

Ingredients:

- 8 oz elbow macaroni
- 2 cups shredded sharp cheddar cheese
- 1 cup shredded mozzarella cheese
- 1 1/2 cups whole milk
- 1/2 cup heavy cream
- 2 tbsp butter
- 1 tbsp flour
- Salt and pepper to taste
- 6 slices bacon, cooked and crumbled
- 1/4 cup breadcrumbs (optional for topping)

Instructions:

1. Cook the elbow macaroni according to package instructions. Drain and set aside.
2. In a large saucepan, melt butter over medium heat. Add the flour and cook for 1 minute.
3. Slowly whisk in milk and cream, cooking until the sauce thickens, about 5 minutes.
4. Stir in the cheddar and mozzarella cheese until melted and smooth.

5. Season with salt and pepper. Add the cooked macaroni to the sauce and stir to combine.

6. Top with crumbled bacon and breadcrumbs (if using). Serve hot.

Grilled Veggie Platter with Hummus

A variety of grilled veggies served with creamy hummus.

Ingredients:

- 1 zucchini, sliced
- 1 eggplant, sliced
- 1 bell pepper, cut into strips
- 1 red onion, sliced
- 1 cup cherry tomatoes
- Olive oil for grilling
- Salt and pepper to taste
- 1 cup hummus (store-bought or homemade)

Instructions:

1. Preheat the grill or grill pan to medium-high heat.
2. Toss the vegetables in olive oil, salt, and pepper.
3. Grill the vegetables, turning occasionally, until tender and slightly charred (about 5-7 minutes per side).
4. Serve the grilled veggies with hummus on the side for dipping.

Carne Asada Burritos

Juicy carne asada wrapped in a warm flour tortilla with fresh toppings.

Ingredients for Carne Asada:

- 1 lb flank steak or skirt steak
- 2 cloves garlic, minced
- 1/4 cup lime juice
- 1/4 cup orange juice
- 1 tbsp soy sauce
- 1 tbsp cumin
- 1 tsp chili powder
- Salt and pepper to taste

Ingredients for Burritos:

- 4 large flour tortillas
- 1 cup cooked rice
- 1 cup shredded lettuce
- 1/2 cup diced tomatoes
- 1/2 cup shredded cheddar cheese
- 1/4 cup sour cream
- 1/4 cup guacamole

Instructions:

1. Marinate the steak in garlic, lime juice, orange juice, soy sauce, cumin, chili powder, salt, and pepper for at least 1 hour.

2. Grill the steak for 4-5 minutes per side or until desired doneness. Let it rest before slicing it thinly.

3. To assemble the burritos, place rice, carne asada, lettuce, tomatoes, cheese, sour cream, and guacamole on each tortilla.

4. Roll up the burritos tightly and serve.

Meatball Sub Sandwiches

Savory meatballs in marinara sauce, topped with melted cheese, all served on a sub roll.

Ingredients:

- 1 lb ground beef
- 1/4 cup breadcrumbs
- 1/4 cup grated parmesan cheese
- 1 egg
- 1 clove garlic, minced
- 1 cup marinara sauce
- 4 sub rolls
- 1 cup shredded mozzarella cheese
- Salt and pepper to taste

Instructions:

1. Preheat oven to 375°F.
2. In a bowl, mix ground beef, breadcrumbs, parmesan cheese, egg, garlic, salt, and pepper. Form into meatballs.
3. Place the meatballs on a baking sheet and bake for 20 minutes, until cooked through.
4. Heat marinara sauce in a large pan and add the cooked meatballs. Simmer for 5 minutes.
5. Split the sub rolls and spoon the meatballs and sauce into each roll. Top with mozzarella cheese.

6. Place in the oven for 5 minutes to melt the cheese. Serve hot.

Spaghetti Carbonara

Creamy pasta with eggs, cheese, and crispy pancetta.

Ingredients:

- 12 oz spaghetti
- 4 oz pancetta, diced
- 2 large eggs
- 1 cup grated parmesan cheese
- 1/2 cup heavy cream (optional)
- 1 clove garlic, minced
- Salt and pepper to taste

Instructions:

1. Cook spaghetti according to package instructions. Reserve 1/2 cup pasta water before draining.
2. While the pasta cooks, sauté the pancetta in a large pan over medium heat until crispy. Add garlic and cook for 1 minute.
3. In a bowl, whisk together eggs, parmesan cheese, and cream (if using).
4. Toss the hot pasta into the pancetta, then pour the egg mixture over the pasta. Stir quickly to coat the pasta, adding reserved pasta water as needed to create a creamy sauce.
5. Season with salt and pepper and serve immediately.

BBQ Ribs with Coleslaw

Tender BBQ ribs served with a tangy, creamy coleslaw.

Ingredients for Ribs:

- 2 racks of baby back ribs
- 1/2 cup BBQ sauce
- 1 tbsp brown sugar
- 1 tbsp paprika
- 1 tsp garlic powder
- Salt and pepper to taste

Ingredients for Coleslaw:

- 4 cups shredded cabbage
- 1 carrot, shredded
- 1/2 cup mayo
- 1 tbsp vinegar
- 1 tbsp sugar
- Salt and pepper to taste

Instructions:

1. Preheat oven to 300°F.
2. Rub the ribs with brown sugar, paprika, garlic powder, salt, and pepper.

3. Wrap the ribs in foil and bake for 2.5-3 hours, until tender.

4. Unwrap the ribs, brush with BBQ sauce, and grill for 5-7 minutes, basting with more sauce.

5. For the coleslaw, mix shredded cabbage, carrot, mayo, vinegar, sugar, salt, and pepper.

6. Serve the ribs with the coleslaw.

Paella

A traditional Spanish rice dish with seafood, chicken, and vegetables.

Ingredients:

- 2 tbsp olive oil
- 1 onion, chopped
- 2 cloves garlic, minced
- 1 bell pepper, chopped
- 1 1/2 cups Arborio rice
- 4 cups chicken broth
- 1/2 cup white wine
- 1/2 tsp saffron (optional)
- 1 lb shrimp, peeled and deveined
- 1/2 lb chicken thighs, diced
- 1/2 cup peas
- 1/2 cup chopped tomatoes
- Lemon wedges for garnish

Instructions:

1. In a large pan, heat olive oil over medium heat. Sauté onions, garlic, and bell pepper until softened.
2. Add rice and cook for 2 minutes. Pour in the wine and cook for 2 more minutes.

3. Add chicken broth, saffron, tomatoes, and chicken. Simmer for 10-12 minutes.

4. Stir in shrimp and peas, cooking for 5-7 minutes until the shrimp is cooked through.

5. Garnish with lemon wedges and serve.

Sweet and Sour Chicken

Crispy chicken tossed in a tangy, sweet sauce with bell peppers and pineapple.

Ingredients for Chicken:

- 1 lb chicken breast, cubed
- 1 cup cornstarch
- 1 egg, beaten
- Oil for frying

Ingredients for Sauce:

- 1/4 cup ketchup
- 1/4 cup vinegar
- 1/4 cup sugar
- 1/4 cup soy sauce
- 1/2 cup pineapple chunks
- 1 bell pepper, chopped

Instructions:

1. Heat oil in a pan and fry the chicken cubes until golden and crispy. Set aside.
2. In a separate pan, mix ketchup, vinegar, sugar, and soy sauce. Cook for 2-3 minutes.
3. Add bell pepper and pineapple chunks, simmering for 5 minutes.
4. Toss the fried chicken in the sweet and sour sauce and serve hot.

Crispy Fish Tacos

Lightly battered fish served in soft tortillas with fresh toppings.

Ingredients for Fish:

- 1 lb white fish fillets (like cod or tilapia)
- 1 cup flour
- 1 tsp paprika
- 1 tsp garlic powder
- 1 egg, beaten
- Oil for frying

Ingredients for Tacos:

- 8 small tortillas
- 1 cup shredded cabbage
- 1/2 cup cilantro, chopped
- 1/4 cup lime juice
- Salsa or hot sauce for topping

Instructions:

1. Mix flour, paprika, garlic powder, and salt. Dip the fish fillets into the egg, then coat with the flour mixture.
2. Fry the fish in hot oil until crispy and golden.

3. Assemble the tacos by placing a piece of fish in each tortilla and topping with shredded cabbage, cilantro, lime juice, and salsa.

4. Serve immediately.

Lobster Rolls

A classic New England-style sandwich filled with tender lobster meat and a creamy dressing.

Ingredients:

- 2 lobster tails (or 1 lb cooked lobster meat)
- 1/4 cup mayonnaise
- 1 tbsp lemon juice
- 1 tbsp fresh parsley, chopped
- 2 tbsp celery, finely diced
- 4 soft rolls or hot dog buns
- 1 tbsp butter, melted
- Salt and pepper to taste

Instructions:

1. Boil the lobster tails in salted water for 5-7 minutes, until cooked. Let cool, then remove the meat and chop into bite-sized pieces.
2. In a bowl, mix mayonnaise, lemon juice, parsley, celery, salt, and pepper.
3. Add the lobster meat to the mayo mixture and stir to combine.
4. Butter the rolls and toast them lightly.
5. Fill the rolls with the lobster mixture and serve immediately.

Baked Ziti with Sausage

A comforting pasta dish with ziti, sausage, marinara sauce, and melted cheese.

Ingredients:

- 1 lb ziti pasta
- 1 lb Italian sausage (mild or spicy)
- 2 cups marinara sauce
- 2 cups ricotta cheese
- 1 1/2 cups shredded mozzarella cheese
- 1/2 cup grated parmesan cheese
- 1/4 cup fresh basil, chopped
- Salt and pepper to taste

Instructions:

1. Preheat the oven to 375°F.
2. Cook the ziti according to package instructions, drain, and set aside.
3. Brown the sausage in a skillet, breaking it into crumbles. Once cooked, add marinara sauce and simmer for 10 minutes.
4. In a baking dish, layer half of the cooked ziti, half of the ricotta, half of the sausage sauce, and half of the mozzarella. Repeat the layers.
5. Top with parmesan cheese and bake for 20-25 minutes, until bubbly and golden.
6. Garnish with fresh basil and serve hot.

Salmon with Avocado Salsa

A light and flavorful dish featuring grilled salmon topped with a fresh avocado salsa.

Ingredients:

- 4 salmon fillets
- 1 tbsp olive oil
- 1 tsp paprika
- Salt and pepper to taste
- 2 avocados, diced
- 1/2 red onion, finely chopped
- 1 small tomato, diced
- 1 tbsp lime juice
- 1/4 cup cilantro, chopped

Instructions:

1. Preheat the grill or skillet to medium-high heat.
2. Rub the salmon fillets with olive oil, paprika, salt, and pepper. Grill for 4-5 minutes per side, until cooked through.
3. In a bowl, combine diced avocados, red onion, tomato, lime juice, and cilantro.
4. Serve the grilled salmon fillets topped with the fresh avocado salsa.

Chicken Parmesan

A crispy chicken cutlet topped with marinara sauce and melted cheese.

Ingredients:

- 4 boneless, skinless chicken breasts
- 1 cup breadcrumbs
- 1/2 cup grated parmesan cheese
- 1 tsp garlic powder
- 2 eggs, beaten
- 1 cup marinara sauce
- 1 1/2 cups shredded mozzarella cheese
- 2 tbsp olive oil
- Salt and pepper to taste

Instructions:

1. Preheat the oven to 375°F.
2. Mix breadcrumbs, parmesan, garlic powder, salt, and pepper in a shallow bowl.
3. Dip the chicken breasts in the beaten eggs, then coat them in the breadcrumb mixture.
4. Heat olive oil in a skillet over medium heat. Cook the chicken for 4-5 minutes per side, until golden and crispy.
5. Transfer the chicken to a baking dish, top with marinara sauce and mozzarella.
6. Bake for 20-25 minutes, until the cheese is melted and bubbly. Serve hot.

Mediterranean Lamb Kebabs

Tender lamb marinated with Mediterranean spices and grilled on skewers.

Ingredients:

- 1 lb lamb, cut into cubes
- 1/4 cup olive oil
- 2 tbsp lemon juice
- 1 tbsp garlic, minced
- 1 tsp dried oregano
- 1 tsp ground cumin
- Salt and pepper to taste
- 1/2 red onion, sliced
- 1 bell pepper, sliced
- 1/2 cup tzatziki sauce (for serving)

Instructions:

1. In a bowl, combine olive oil, lemon juice, garlic, oregano, cumin, salt, and pepper.
2. Add the lamb cubes to the marinade and let it sit for at least 1 hour (or overnight).
3. Thread the lamb onto skewers, alternating with onion and bell pepper.
4. Grill the kebabs over medium-high heat for 4-5 minutes per side, until the lamb reaches your desired level of doneness.
5. Serve with tzatziki sauce.

Goulash

A hearty Hungarian stew made with beef, paprika, and vegetables.

Ingredients:

- 1 lb beef stew meat, cubed
- 1 onion, chopped
- 2 cloves garlic, minced
- 1 tbsp paprika
- 1/2 tsp caraway seeds
- 4 cups beef broth
- 2 carrots, chopped
- 2 potatoes, peeled and diced
- Salt and pepper to taste
- 1 tbsp flour (optional, for thickening)

Instructions:

1. Heat oil in a large pot over medium heat. Brown the beef on all sides, then remove and set aside.
2. In the same pot, sauté the onion and garlic until softened.
3. Add the paprika and caraway seeds, cooking for 1 minute.
4. Return the beef to the pot, add broth, carrots, potatoes, salt, and pepper. Bring to a simmer.

5. Cook for 1-1.5 hours, until the beef is tender. If you'd like a thicker stew, mix flour with water and stir it into the pot.

6. Serve hot.

Beef Wellington

A show-stopping dish featuring beef tenderloin coated in mushroom duxelles and puff pastry.

Ingredients:

- 1 lb beef tenderloin, trimmed
- 2 tbsp olive oil
- 2 cups mushrooms, finely chopped
- 1 tbsp butter
- 2 cloves garlic, minced
- 1/4 cup dry white wine
- 1/4 cup Dijon mustard
- 1 package puff pastry (enough to wrap the beef)
- 1 egg, beaten
- Salt and pepper to taste

Instructions:

1. Preheat the oven to 400°F.
2. Sear the beef tenderloin in a hot pan with olive oil, cooking for 2-3 minutes on each side. Brush with mustard.
3. In a pan, cook the mushrooms, garlic, and butter until the mushrooms release their liquid. Add wine and cook until dry.
4. Roll out the puff pastry on a floured surface. Spread the mushroom mixture over the pastry. Place the beef in the center and wrap it in the pastry.

5. Brush with egg wash and bake for 25-30 minutes, until golden brown.

6. Let rest before slicing and serving.

Cajun Jambalaya

A classic Creole dish with rice, sausage, chicken, shrimp, and bold Cajun spices.

Ingredients:

- 1 lb sausage, sliced
- 1 lb chicken breast, cubed
- 1 lb shrimp, peeled and deveined
- 1 onion, chopped
- 1 bell pepper, chopped
- 2 celery stalks, chopped
- 3 cloves garlic, minced
- 1 can diced tomatoes (14 oz)
- 2 cups chicken broth
- 1 1/2 cups long-grain rice
- 2 tbsp Cajun seasoning
- Salt and pepper to taste

Instructions:

1. In a large pot, cook sausage until browned. Add chicken and cook until browned.
2. Add onion, bell pepper, celery, and garlic. Cook until softened.
3. Stir in tomatoes, chicken broth, rice, Cajun seasoning, salt, and pepper. Bring to a boil.

4. Reduce heat, cover, and simmer for 20-25 minutes, until the rice is tender.

5. Add shrimp, cover, and cook for an additional 5 minutes. Serve hot.

Spicy BBQ Pulled Chicken Nachos

Crispy tortilla chips topped with spicy BBQ pulled chicken, melted cheese, and fresh toppings.

Ingredients:

- 2 chicken breasts, cooked and shredded
- 1/2 cup BBQ sauce
- 1 bag tortilla chips
- 2 cups shredded cheddar cheese
- 1/2 cup sour cream
- 1/4 cup jalapeños, sliced
- 1/2 red onion, diced
- 1/4 cup cilantro, chopped

Instructions:

1. Preheat the oven to 375°F.
2. Toss shredded chicken with BBQ sauce.
3. On a baking sheet, spread tortilla chips. Top with BBQ chicken and shredded cheese.
4. Bake for 10-12 minutes, until the cheese is melted.
5. Top with sour cream, jalapeños, onion, and cilantro. Serve hot.

Mushroom Risotto

A creamy Italian rice dish made with mushrooms and Parmesan.

Ingredients:

- 1 1/2 cups Arborio rice
- 4 cups chicken or vegetable broth
- 1 cup mushrooms, sliced
- 1/2 cup white wine
- 1/2 cup grated Parmesan cheese
- 1 tbsp butter
- 1 onion, chopped
- 2 cloves garlic, minced
- Salt and pepper to taste

Instructions:

1. Heat butter in a large pan and sauté the onions and garlic until softened.
2. Add mushrooms and cook until they release their moisture.
3. Stir in the rice and cook for 1-2 minutes, coating it with the butter.
4. Gradually add the wine, then the broth, one cup at a time, stirring frequently until the liquid is absorbed before adding more.
5. Cook for 20-25 minutes, until the rice is tender. Stir in Parmesan, salt, and pepper. Serve hot.

Grilled Shrimp Skewers

Juicy, marinated shrimp grilled to perfection on skewers.

Ingredients:

- 1 lb large shrimp, peeled and deveined
- 2 tbsp olive oil
- 2 tbsp lemon juice
- 2 cloves garlic, minced
- 1 tsp smoked paprika
- Salt and pepper to taste
- Skewers (soak in water if wooden)

Instructions:

1. In a bowl, combine olive oil, lemon juice, garlic, paprika, salt, and pepper.
2. Toss shrimp in marinade and chill for 20–30 minutes.
3. Thread shrimp onto skewers.
4. Grill over medium-high heat for 2–3 minutes per side until pink and slightly charred.
5. Serve hot with lemon wedges.

Spicy Chicken Wings

Oven-baked wings with a spicy, crispy finish.

Ingredients:

- 2 lbs chicken wings
- 2 tbsp olive oil
- 1 tsp garlic powder
- 1 tsp paprika
- 1/2 tsp cayenne pepper
- Salt and pepper to taste
- 1/4 cup hot sauce (like Frank's)
- 2 tbsp melted butter

Instructions:

1. Preheat oven to 425°F.
2. Toss wings with oil and spices.
3. Spread on a baking sheet and bake for 40–45 minutes, flipping halfway.
4. Mix hot sauce and butter, then toss baked wings in sauce.
5. Serve with ranch or blue cheese.

Baked Sweet Potatoes with Sour Cream

A simple and satisfying side or light meal.

Ingredients:

- 4 medium sweet potatoes
- 1/2 cup sour cream
- 2 tbsp green onions, sliced
- Salt and pepper to taste

Instructions:

1. Preheat oven to 400°F.
2. Wash and pierce sweet potatoes. Bake for 45–60 minutes until tender.
3. Slice open and fluff the insides with a fork.
4. Top with sour cream, green onions, salt, and pepper.

Grilled Flatbreads with Pesto

Charred flatbread topped with herby pesto and optional extras.

Ingredients:

- 4 flatbreads or naan
- 1/2 cup pesto
- 1/4 cup grated Parmesan
- Optional: cherry tomatoes, mozzarella, arugula

Instructions:

1. Preheat grill or grill pan to medium-high.
2. Grill flatbreads for 1–2 minutes per side until lightly charred.
3. Spread with pesto, sprinkle with Parmesan, and add any toppings.
4. Return to grill for 1 minute to warm. Slice and serve.

Philly Cheesesteak Sandwiches

Thinly sliced beef, onions, and melty cheese on a hoagie roll.

Ingredients:

- 1 lb ribeye or flank steak, thinly sliced
- 1 onion, sliced
- 1 green pepper (optional), sliced
- 4 hoagie rolls
- 8 slices provolone cheese
- 1 tbsp oil
- Salt and pepper to taste

Instructions:

1. Sauté onions (and peppers if using) in oil until soft. Set aside.
2. Cook steak slices over high heat, season with salt and pepper.
3. Return veggies to pan, place cheese over top, and let it melt.
4. Spoon mixture into hoagie rolls and serve hot.

Steak and Potato Salad

A hearty salad with grilled steak, crispy potatoes, and vinaigrette.

Ingredients:

- 1 lb steak (sirloin or flank)
- 2 cups baby potatoes, halved
- 4 cups mixed greens
- 1/2 cup cherry tomatoes, halved
- 1/4 red onion, thinly sliced
- 2 tbsp olive oil
- Salt, pepper, and balsamic vinaigrette

Instructions:

1. Roast potatoes at 425°F for 25 minutes until golden.
2. Grill or pan-sear steak to preferred doneness, rest, then slice.
3. Toss greens with tomatoes, onion, vinaigrette, and potatoes.
4. Top with sliced steak and serve.

Classic Beef Burgers

Juicy, flavorful burgers grilled or pan-fried to perfection.

Ingredients:

- 1 lb ground beef (80/20)
- Salt and pepper
- 4 burger buns
- Optional: cheese, lettuce, tomato, pickles, ketchup, mustard

Instructions:

1. Form beef into 4 patties. Season with salt and pepper.
2. Grill or pan-fry over medium-high heat, 3–4 minutes per side.
3. Add cheese in the last minute if desired.
4. Toast buns, assemble burgers with toppings, and serve.

Shrimp Scampi

Succulent shrimp sautéed in a garlic butter wine sauce, served over pasta.

Ingredients:

- 1 lb shrimp, peeled and deveined
- 3 tbsp butter
- 3 cloves garlic, minced
- 1/4 tsp red pepper flakes
- 1/4 cup white wine or chicken broth
- 1 tbsp lemon juice
- 8 oz linguine or spaghetti
- Parsley and Parmesan for garnish

Instructions:

1. Cook pasta according to package instructions.
2. In a skillet, melt butter, add garlic and red pepper flakes, sauté briefly.
3. Add shrimp, cook 1–2 minutes per side until pink.
4. Add wine and lemon juice, simmer 2 minutes.
5. Toss with cooked pasta, garnish, and serve hot.

Veggie Pizza

Colorful pizza loaded with fresh vegetables and melty cheese.

Ingredients:

- 1 pizza dough (store-bought or homemade)
- 1/2 cup pizza sauce
- 1 1/2 cups shredded mozzarella
- Toppings: bell peppers, mushrooms, olives, onions, spinach, tomatoes

Instructions:

1. Preheat oven to 475°F. Roll out dough on a floured surface.
2. Spread sauce, sprinkle cheese, and add veggies.
3. Bake for 12–15 minutes until crust is golden and cheese is bubbly.
4. Slice and serve.

Steak Tacos with Guacamole

Juicy grilled steak tucked into tortillas with fresh guac.

Ingredients:

- 1 lb flank or skirt steak
- 1 tsp chili powder
- 1/2 tsp cumin
- Salt and pepper
- 8 small tortillas
- 1 cup guacamole
- Optional: onions, cilantro, salsa

Instructions:

1. Season steak with chili powder, cumin, salt, and pepper.
2. Grill or pan-sear to preferred doneness. Let rest and slice thinly.
3. Warm tortillas.
4. Fill with steak, guacamole, and toppings of choice.

Tomato Basil Soup with Grilled Cheese

A comforting, creamy soup paired with golden, melty sandwiches.

Ingredients (Soup):

- 2 tbsp olive oil
- 1 onion, chopped
- 3 cloves garlic, minced
- 2 cans (28 oz) crushed tomatoes
- 2 cups vegetable broth
- 1/2 cup heavy cream
- Salt, pepper, and sugar to taste
- 1/2 cup fresh basil leaves

Instructions:

1. Sauté onion in olive oil until soft. Add garlic and cook 1 minute.
2. Stir in tomatoes and broth. Simmer for 20 minutes.
3. Blend until smooth (optional), then stir in cream, salt, pepper, sugar, and basil. Simmer 5 more minutes.

Grilled Cheese:

- Butter 8 slices of bread.
- Place cheese (like cheddar or mozzarella) between 2 slices, buttered sides out.
- Grill in a pan until golden and melty on both sides.

Chicken and Dumplings

Creamy stew with fluffy, tender dumplings.

Ingredients:

- 1 tbsp butter
- 1 onion, chopped
- 2 carrots, sliced
- 2 celery stalks, sliced
- 1 tsp thyme
- 4 cups chicken broth
- 2 cups cooked shredded chicken
- 1/2 cup cream

Dumplings:

- 1 cup flour
- 2 tsp baking powder
- 1/2 tsp salt
- 2 tbsp butter
- 1/2 cup milk

Instructions:

1. In a pot, sauté onion, carrots, and celery in butter until soft.

2. Add thyme, broth, and chicken. Bring to a boil, then reduce heat.

3. Mix dumpling ingredients until a sticky dough forms.

4. Drop spoonfuls onto simmering soup. Cover and cook for 15 minutes.

5. Stir in cream and serve warm.

Slow-Cooker Chili

Deep, hearty chili perfect for lazy days.

Ingredients:

- 1 lb ground beef or turkey
- 1 onion, chopped
- 3 cloves garlic, minced
- 1 can (15 oz) black beans
- 1 can (15 oz) kidney beans
- 1 can (28 oz) diced tomatoes
- 2 tbsp tomato paste
- 2 tbsp chili powder
- 1 tsp cumin
- Salt and pepper to taste

Instructions:

1. Brown meat with onion and garlic in a skillet, then transfer to slow cooker.
2. Add remaining ingredients and stir.
3. Cook on low for 6–8 hours or high for 3–4 hours.
4. Serve with sour cream, cheese, and cornbread.

Beef Tostadas

Crunchy tostadas topped with flavorful beef and fresh toppings.

Ingredients:

- 1 lb ground beef
- 1 tsp cumin
- 1 tsp chili powder
- 1/2 tsp paprika
- Salt and pepper
- 8 tostada shells
- Refried beans (optional)
- Toppings: lettuce, tomato, cheese, avocado, sour cream, salsa

Instructions:

1. Cook beef in a skillet with seasonings until browned.
2. Spread beans on tostadas, if using.
3. Add beef and top with your favorite fixings.
4. Serve immediately for crunch!

Ramen with Soft-Boiled Eggs

Quick and flavorful ramen enhanced with jammy eggs.

Ingredients:

- 2 ramen packs (discard seasoning packets)
- 4 cups broth (chicken or vegetable)
- 1 tbsp soy sauce
- 1 tsp sesame oil
- 1 tsp grated ginger
- 2 soft-boiled eggs (boil for 6–7 min, then chill & peel)
- Toppings: green onions, mushrooms, bok choy, seaweed, chili oil

Instructions:

1. In a pot, heat broth, soy sauce, sesame oil, and ginger.
2. Add mushrooms or veggies if using, simmer until tender.
3. Add noodles and cook per package directions.
4. Ladle into bowls and top with halved eggs and toppings.

Loaded Baked Potatoes

Fluffy potatoes packed with savory toppings.

Ingredients:

- 4 large russet potatoes
- Olive oil & salt (for baking)
- Toppings: shredded cheddar, bacon bits, sour cream, green onions, butter, steamed broccoli, etc.

Instructions:

1. Preheat oven to 400°F (200°C). Scrub potatoes, dry, rub with oil and salt.
2. Bake for 50–60 minutes until tender.
3. Slice open, fluff inside with a fork, and load up your toppings.

Banh Mi Sandwiches (Vietnam)

French baguette meets Southeast Asian flavor.

Ingredients:

- 1 baguette, split
- Grilled pork, chicken, or tofu
- Pickled carrots & daikon (1:1 vinegar, sugar, and water soak)
- Cucumber slices, cilantro, jalapeño slices
- Mayo or sriracha mayo

Instructions:

1. Toast baguette lightly.
2. Spread mayo, add protein, and layer with pickles, cucumber, cilantro, and jalapeños.
3. Serve with a cold drink and crunchy chips!

Carne Asada Fries

The ultimate indulgent snack or meal.

Ingredients:

- Frozen or homemade fries
- Carne asada (grilled marinated flank steak, sliced)
- Shredded cheese
- Guacamole, sour cream, pico de gallo, jalapeños

Instructions:

1. Cook fries until golden.
2. Top with sliced carne asada and cheese—broil for 1–2 min to melt.
3. Add guac, sour cream, and extras. Grab a fork!

Stuffed Bell Peppers

Healthy, hearty, and customizable.

Ingredients:

- 4 large bell peppers, halved or tops cut off & seeds removed
- 1 lb ground beef or turkey
- 1 cup cooked rice or quinoa
- 1/2 onion, chopped
- 1 cup tomato sauce
- 1 tsp garlic, salt, pepper
- Cheese for topping

Instructions:

1. Sauté onion and meat, season, stir in rice and sauce.
2. Stuff into peppers, place in baking dish.
3. Top with cheese and bake at 375°F (190°C) for 30–35 minutes.

Grilled Cheese with Tomato Jam

Sweet, savory twist on the classic.

Ingredients (Tomato Jam):

- 2 cups cherry or roma tomatoes, chopped
- 1/4 cup sugar
- 1 tbsp vinegar
- Pinch of chili flakes & salt

Jam Instructions:

1. Simmer ingredients until thick, about 30–40 min.

Grilled Cheese:

- Buttered bread slices + sharp cheddar or gouda
- Grill on pan until crispy and golden
- Add a layer of tomato jam for magic.

Chicken Shawarma Wraps

Middle Eastern spice in a handheld package.

Ingredients:

- Chicken thighs, marinated in:
    - 2 tbsp yogurt
    - 1 tbsp lemon juice
    - 1 tsp cumin, paprika, turmeric, garlic, cinnamon, salt
- Pita or flatbread
- Garlic sauce or tzatziki
- Lettuce, tomato, onion, cucumber

Instructions:

1. Marinate chicken for 1+ hour, then grill or pan-fry until browned.
2. Slice and wrap in warm pita with veggies and sauce.
3. Optional: a drizzle of hot sauce or hummus!

www.ingramcontent.com/pod-product-compliance
Lightning Source LLC
LaVergne TN
LVHW081318060526
838201LV00055B/2346